HOUSE

HOUSE

Mariela Griffor

Mayapple Press, 2007

Copyright © Mariela Griffor, 2007
All rights reserved.

Published by   Mayapple Press
                408 N. Lincoln St.
                Bay City, MI 48708
                www.mayapplepress.com

ISBN 978-0932412-539

Cover and book designed and typeset by Judith Kerman in Garamond. Cover photograph, "Mid-Michigan Palm," and author photograph by Ian Tadashi Moore.

Acknowledgements:

With deep gratitude to Fraser Sutherland and Judith Kerman for editing this book, to Judith Kerman's Mayapple Press for publishing this collection.

The Frank and Carol Hennessy Award from the Grosse Pointe Artists Association helped me to complete this book, for which I am grateful.

Joyful thanks to my fellow poets and writers Jorge Etcheverry who published many of these poems in Spanish translation in *La Cita Trunca*, and Camilo Marks who rescued the Spanish voice in my work.

Respect and gratitude to Ambassador José Miguel Cruz who returned me to my past and put Chile back in my life.

Distributed by:
Small Press Distribution
1341 Seventh Street
Berkeley, CA 94710-1409
1-800-869-7553
and
Partners Book Distributing
2325 Jarco Dr.
Holt, MI 48842
1-800-336-3137
and
Wayne State University Press
The Leonard N. Simons Building
4809 Woodward Avenue, Detroit, MI 48201-1309
1-800-978-7323

What we love is your peace, not your mask. Your warrior's face is not handsome. North America, you are handsome and spacious.

Pablo Neruda
"I Wish the Woodcutter Would Wake Up"
translated by Robert Bly

For Grandfather

Contents

HOUSE
Prologue — 5
One: They — 6
Two: Poems That Contradict Each Other — 7
Three: Either-Or — 8
Four: Requiem, *or* The Time Before the Dice Fall — 9
Five: In a Dream with Neruda — 10
Six: Song for Chile — 11
Seven: Song of Goodbye — 13
Eight: Kiss — 15
Nine: On a Quiet Summer's Night — 16
Ten: Remember the Ten Commandments — 17
Eleven: It Comes from the Depths of the Earth — 18
Twelve: First Guesthouse — 19
Thirteen: Rising — 20
Fourteen: Beyond the Red Traffic Light — 21
Fifteen: Futuristic — 22
Sixteen: If You Are Sad, Leave the Country — 23
Seventeen: Santiago Revisited — 24
Poem Without a Number: House — 26
Eighteen: Years of Marriage — 27
Nineteen: Webster's — 28
Twenty: Husband — 29
Twenty-One: War and Peace — 30
Twenty-Two: For the Van Pelts — 31
Twenty-Three: Hyperemesis — 32
Twenty-Four: Balance — 33
Twenty-Five: For R.G. — 34
Twenty-Six: Pure Math — 35
Twenty-Seven: Memories — 36
Twenty-Eight: Details — 38
Twenty-Nine: Yellow Ribbons — 39
Thirty: Just in Time — 41
Conclusion — 42

GUESTHOUSE
Hair of Sand — 45

Notes — 48
About the Author — 49

HOUSE

Prologue

The gods can't
speak in tongues.

The gods do and undo.
They don't think.

They don't speak
the language
of humans.

One: They

They broke the fingers
of those who didn't want to shoot people.
Those who could sing and play the guitar had their hands cut off.

They cut open the stomachs of politicians
so they would sink fast into our cold ocean.

They opened five torture chambers across the country:
Quiriquina, Tejas Verdes,
República, Villa Grimaldi, The Parral House.

The names became as familiar as our wines.

They did it in the name of God.

De la memoria perdida
acercándose
poco a poco

Two: Poems That Contradict Each Other

After the film Nacht und Nebel, directed by Alain Resnais

1.

Last night I had nightmares again.
I dreamt of a head without its right eye in a pile of human heads.
Bodies in graves and the boots of soldiers.

The madness of a society in fear provokes these horrors.
They did what they did because they could. (Haven't you heard this before?)

But that is not the whole truth.

2.

The difference between two who both can do evil
yet one chooses not to
is based on the latter's belief that life can be better.

You don't understand, it is both good and bad.
Good, you can still dream at night and feel whole.
Bad, you can never understand the victims of such horrors.
In the end, we are still alive with nightmares or without them.
Evil has no measure, kindness and goodness don't either.
We can never escape our past.
At least, not with a good movie and popcorn on a Saturday night.

media somñolienta
y llena de polvo
viene

Three: Either-Or

For Pablo Neruda

Facing the sea from your house in Isla Negra
and odes to the life we know,
with your feet sunken in the sand,
with a summer hat shielding your face
and caracolas flourishing their tails in the air,
we see you.

Everything comes to an end

but not you,
who taught us there is more hope
in eel soup than in the promises governments want us to buy.

You who never talked to God but to people
bring me back to Chillán.
Your poems
remind me
a part of me's
still there.
Even if I never left.

mi lengua maternal
a traerme
recuerdos gratos

Four: Requiem, *or* The Time Before the Dice Fall

It is difficult to believe that you are gone.

With you, a piece of my good side also left.
It was not difficult to be good alongside you.

I felt tranquil, protected, and secure
when I could hear your footsteps.

While you were fighting for more life,
I was fighting the tyrants.

Claudia, Aunt Claudia, clear as a mirror.
We were separated on the first day of October.

It wasn't easy to get used, after you died,
to ill-fated meetings. Exile was necessary.

Now it's nothing to worry about.
Cancer eats away from within.

They didn't tell me how to avoid suffering.
Now that you are not here
I have the best of you:

The goodness in you
fills the window of my memories.

Hit me hard and tell me that you are not dead.
Five years is nothing, five deaths is too much.

When I count one, two, three, four,
the tears come forth to greet you,

Claudia, Aunt Claudia,
enigmatic face of my tender years.

olores violentos
palabras tímidas

Five: In a Dream with Neruda

I remembered you when
I tried to remember happiness,
the anxiety in my eyes and in my hands
when I tried to memorize your poetry.
I repeated it many times until
I forgot what I said.

The teacher is counting the minutes.
To feel the eyes of my classmates
makes me shake,
no place for so much cowardice,

my body was so tiny, my prayers for help
with the eyes of my classmates upon me
disappeared.

I remained alone
saying, "Walking around …

"Walking around

"Walking around

Walking around" by Neruda

and I vanished.

susurros de hombre
en mis oidos
campanas en un mar abierto

Six: Song for Chile

So many days of restlessness
between the bars of ferocious forgetting.

So many kisses and furtive embraces,
they open their graves and disappear.

Thousands of words, sweet melodies.

Images full of horror, full of furies.

Words that limit my destiny,
my dreams, my craziness.

Words that symbolize the
meaning of our existence
become bubbles
one morning

The colors of dusk degrading in the west of the universe,
the dark red of fright and hope.

Everything I love nearby and in the distance,
everything has gone to a tiny place, remote,
where you, like a miracle,
appear five seconds each daybreak.

I carry you like a white shirt,
perfumed,
that brings me
pride and praises.

I take you
and caress you
and I hide you
in my sacred ritual, where
you will come to relieve me
of pain, to help me in disillusionment.
Return to me as fresh as before the evil covered us.

I will keep you close and protected.
I will polish you for five seconds every dawn,
clothe you in fine colors
that will illuminate you in the distance.

I will give you all my honors
and I will love you forever.

vientos del sur y azucenas
viene mi lengua materna

Seven: Song of Goodbye

I leave with the train
that destiny prepared for me.
Cars take me away from you
in the rapid zigzag of your white legs.
I'm trying to capture in a glance
the slow movement of my poplars.
I leave softly, without reproach and nostalgia,
without the immeasurable fear
of not seeing you again.

The coat of skin that protects me is white, blue, and red
full of images that remind me of you.
New hills and mountains.
In my soul's dry hope of meeting again, I will wait.

In the nakedness of my baggage, the sacred memories
I treasure day by day, kiss by kiss,
I will hang above my door.

And if some day your ocean cries out
it is because I think of you.
If your mountains tumble with the howls of an injured woman
it is because my assassin nostalgia thinks of you.
Your streets suddenly turn with autumn colors.
I run in my exile like someone crazed,
suddenly I think of you.
Don't forget me, I don't forget.
I don't abandon you.
I will board train compartments that smell of your eucalyptus,
your bridges of beautiful words,
your clouds that will bring back my youth,
marred by black lamps.

Even if you are sad
I am thinking of you.

The train that will take me away is constructed by hands
full of the soft mumbling of worlds gone by,
like going to a subterranean world.

I will return pure and fresh, as we were before tyrants.
I don't forget you,
my stubborn mind will wait for our meeting.
All this time will pass rapidly.
When in the end I can open your door again,
we will merge.

cargada de nostalgia
como siempre

Eight: Kiss

My most precious landscape has the colors of autumn.
Along Forestal Park we walk as in old good times.
Children playing reminds me of our own childhoods
when you and I awaited each other.

Your pains will be healed,
sorrows will disappear into air,
melancholic nostalgia will turn into slow wanderings on
the road toward valleys and hills.
Your hands will be relieved of their chains.
Rivers will be consoled and will turn
into silent witnesses.

Let the autumn come and let memories of you visit my pillows.
Come back to this earth with your smile
to create new desires with your beautiful dark eyes.
I wait for you in the sleep of each night.
Despite the years your mouth is still honey.
We will see each other in the air.
This road is long.
Don't leave me alone until then.

a dejarme
un paquete de días de lluvia

Nine: On a Quiet Summer's Night

On a quiet summer's night
when I was counting stars,
the short figure of Elena surprised me
and said to me: *If you continue bothering those stars,*
warts are going to cover your hands!
I thought those things never happened.
I continued to count
one by one
all those beauties
and the next day
the first itching on my right hand began.
I was afraid of bothering the stars.
Thirty years have passed since.
I look at the dark blue of the sky
and without wanting to I count slowly,
provocatively, up to fifty, and I stop.
I pray to Saint Therese not to punish me.
I don't have bad intentions.
I pray to her not to send me warts.
I promise her to look at the sky and keep quiet, not to count,
not to make one sound to bother the stars,
all those beauties
blinking their eyes
in the sky.

cuerpos calientes
al frente de una chimenea
viene calmada con su pelo de arena

Ten: Remember the Ten Commandments

> *Purity to the pure.*
> *Anonymous*

The hour of final judgment has come.
The time has come
to tell all of our secrets,
to fear the hand of God.

Like a flock of virgin lambs we huddle
to give one another warmth and comfort.
We are waiting for the sacred host and the blood
that we will drink to purify our fearful souls.

Have we offended You?
Have we forgotten You?
Have compassion for our voice.
Yesterday bandits came upon our village
and killed us in body, in spirit,
without shame, with revenge, with pain.
Give us peace, calm, reconciliation.

The time has come to start a new way,
to extend our hands
and apply what we know:
where there is no forgiveness, there is no forgetting.
This is what God teaches.

Protect those who survived.
Bless anew everything.

Show us the immanent life of our land on fire,
let fall Your fury, let us fear Your hand,
the time has come to mend everything that was broken,
the time has come to be alone with You.

con su boca de mar
con sus caricias en tinieblas
viene y me canta estos versos

Eleven: It Comes from the Depths of the Earth

For H.I.

From the depths of the earth
comes the morena undulating slowly.
She comes with her taste of honey
with her contagious smile
moving her hips sensually, rhythmically,
with her sigh and perfumed breath.
She conquers the mulato
before the distrustful ocean.

Born there from the sand
from the jubilant silence
from the southern rural skies
from San Pedro Victoriano
the child of the morenos
who will roam the earth
without rest.

Without regret
without astonishment
the mulata leaves the mulato
pondering in disenchantment:
How can I go back and see her and have her close
heal the scars of her leaving
if I love her so much.

para aplacar mi tristeza
viene dulce y fuerte
con sílabas que reconozco

Twelve: First Guesthouse

I believe one day the distance between myself and God will disappear.
Franz Wright

I hate Swedish meatballs,
especially with *lingonsylt.*
It was my first meal at the refugee camp.

Halstahammar was like a Christmas postcard,
snowy, with small red houses along the road.
My hair broke in the cold weather of 1985.

Swedish meatballs remind me of a time
when life was alienation,
a time of looking for God and
not finding Him.

No matter what you try, nothing
will change.
I crossed the Atlantic for the first time.
A blond, blue-eyed policeman asked:
Political afiliation?
None. I said three times.

Two big Dobermans sniffed
around me while another man
stamped my passport.

con sonidos de delicia
con voces de arroyo
viene y le rindo mi homenaje

Thirteen: Rising

I speak to You God for only one reason: fear.

Fear of Your busy schedule.

With rifles in one hand,
stones in the other.

Their revenge, their greediness
for goods.
A shot hits me in the center of the heart and I cannot
not see You.

Fear invades me and shakes my hand.
I make the sign of the cross.
I cannot see Your face or Your eyes,
even hear Your words.

I can only sense this pain,
myself diminutive under
the blue sky filled with stars.

como reina en su palacio
le doy mis más
preciados tesoros

Fourteen: Beyond the Red Traffic Light

What I have within
moves the brain and the guts,
makes me cry.
It makes me want
to disembowel the universe,
to see if something changes,
if so much pain
passes with the wind.

I lost my refuge among mines, mountains, jails,
lakes, secret bases, red oceans.

The place where I was born is lost.
Money does me no good.
You are gone,
and I remain anticipating long winters.

I lost my place,
the refuges of my nation are lost.
Rebellion is what I possess.

The green light saves me again.

frases de lamentos
carcajadas frescas
ramilletes de violetas

Fifteen: Futuristic

I try to forget
that I come from another America.
The masochist within makes me turn to my lost roots,
like a tornado, a passion I pretend to forget
that jumps into the shadows.

The magic of a half-awakened moon remains.
This love that made us ill
will last until the end of our days.
Life begins and ends on the same day.
No one shares it, it has turned into a utopia.
Everything is covered with lies,
the categories have changed.
Principles are like coals turning into ashes
in an open fire.
To defend life stubbornly has lost its value.
To live without life is not absurd.

The volcanoes are covered with yellow and black,
each one absolute every time it explodes.
The bridges of words are broken
one by one on the way to hell.
Not even limbo exists according to the Pope.
The poor kill each other,
a permanent condition.

We are tired.
No trees to protect us,
dried blood lies in the swamps,
blood drenches the nation.
Time has changed everything,
we belong to another generation,
another America.
We will meet with ancient souls
whether the North wants them or not.

compradas en Huérfanos
el aire marino
la arena negra de San Pedro

Sixteen: If You Are Sad, Leave the Country

Sometimes it is difficult for me
to explain why I left Chile
the first time.

I say,
I needed a pause,
to start again,
to forget the rendevous with Simon at the Normandy cinema,
pretending to be a couple,
learning new codenames every month.
I was saturated with Santiago,
the allergies wouldn't leave me.
It was difficult to stay healthy.

I went far.
Brazil was dangerous in a different way.

We arrived in Rio
and life changed completely.
Nothing left of the way it was.
I felt almost relieved.

I kept myself from becoming sad so quickly.
I surprised myself.

el robusto silbido del viento
el color rojo oscuro
de los atardeceres en Santiago

Seventeen: Santiago Revisited

For Fabiola

I thought about you the other night.
The polluted air and the cold on the street
did not prevent people walking in unknown directions.
The smell from a restaurant reminded me
of the Chinese place on the corner of
Brazil and Compania, a place
where our student pockets
would quickly satisfy our aching stomachs.

Life has evolved,
sometimes kind, sometimes unkind,
like all lives.

How and when do women like you find their men?
With silent envy I could see your patience.
I knew you would wait for him.
How long would it take? One or many years?
Could you live in that constant waiting?
Could you handle the void until then?
It is not easy to think about you
and compare you with other women I know.

They were married in church with their papers in order,
you barely a man's concubine.
They think about blood once a month,
you see blood every time a comrade's shot down.
Even in you, when a bullet
went straight through your black "napa" boots
and you didn't feel anything until hours later,
the adrenaline was too high, you told me then.
How can women like you return to suburban life
talking to other women about French doors?

Suicide becomes an option.
Not because you miss the time of struggle
but because of a senseless French door.
Would you agree?

I think about you and I ask myself
who taught you not to fear
the General, the uniform, the fences, the tanks,
the curfew, the gleaming Uzi each soldier bears.
How could a tiny girl from this surrealist city
possibly believe she could change the world?

I remember again your words:
"General: Your orders die everyday,
my conviction grows like a Victor Jara song.
We will see who will win, I will attack you every time
one of your soldiers takes a piss."
The laughter of others was part of the song.
It is not easy to live up to your standard.

Suburban life is a bastard,
full of duties, a picturesque pattern of mortification
of the flesh by eating and fasting.
It is easy to get lost, especially if you are not around
to keep me straight.
Would I dare to put a picture of you on my piano
and explain to whoever asks
who you were
and who you are now?
Could I tell them
you were the only woman selected to kill the General?
No others had the honor.
Or that you waited for your lover five years
totally faithful to his soul and body?
Could they understand what faithful means?

palabras de amor
dichas en voz muy baja
y de nuevo el sonido del mar

Poem Without a Number: House

In this house,
covered to the ceiling with my insomnia,
spilling the evil
of a complex journey,
I remember:
A barricade. A homemade bomb
made by my hands,
the image of my lover and
in my head a semi-automatic
as redemption.

I beg forgiveness of all of you.
The rain is too thin to stop the fire.

My legs and arms are heavy.
Behind me, Santiago blazes
and bullets whiz at the sight of who we were,
ancestral pain I cannot shake off.
His body disappears from the earth into the air.
A heart spattered in the streets follows me in my defeat.

I think
about you and
my house on fire,
the vision of my father fallen to his knees
praying for a miracle while
the rain disappears
in front of me.

en la Isla Quiriquina
el sumbido de las caracolas
anterior a llegada de los soldados

Eighteen: Years of Marriage

You bastard! You did it again,
you crawled into your child's eyes
and extracted my pity.

My heart is tired of reminiscences
of bitter lips.

I was left empty without my colors.
I condemn you for this mistrust.

I will conjure your absence
calling it from this exile.
I dream about the silence
that will protect me from your madness.

el sonido de una isla
sin camaras de tortura y el joven y atractivo Capitán
enamorando a mi prima

Nineteen: Webster's

This is a love affair.

One in which I try
to conquer.
It's not a simple one.
We feel attracted to our spiral curse.
We are so different.

I dream in codes with sounds and syllables of churches,
he dreams noises
from purgatory, from hell.
We like each other.

I don't remember when it started:
In my sophomore year, my English teacher
translated for me all the Frank Sinatra songs.

A German boy
kissed me and introduced me to the songs of Holly Cole.
He didn't speak Spanish, I didn't speak German.
That night I heard for the first time "I love you"
even though someone had said those words before.

el primer beso de la secundaria
en las orillas del Río Mapocho
el frente del parque Forestal

Twenty: Husband

Together as before, we are leaning
into the center of our bed, every day aware of
what we did to each other. Testing the ways of an incessant renewal.
Sometimes tenderness comes to the rescue.
I, obedient, follow the path to the frivolity of our senses
and ask a simple question before I fall asleep:
Don't you ever get tired of being a dreamer?

I never get tired.

Now shut your mouth and let me sleep.

viene esta lengua gigante
y me arrebata el cuerpo,
me submerge en un sonido

Twenty-one: War and Peace

Woman 1: Poor girls, their fathers suddenly went to heaven.

Woman 2: Pick your man,
don't let him go to war.

Woman 3: How long should women wait
so their fathers' dreams can flourish?

de catástrofes humanas
me arrebata el corazón
con un cuchillo sangriento

Twenty-two: For the Van Pelts

Her wedding was on time.
She and Don stood at the entrance of the
Historical Village in Plymouth.

She was wearing a dress, a bouquet of beige roses.
The dress matched the color of the roses.
The music, a harp.
All our grown children
spread across the room.
Pilar and Christian, Manuel and
Shirley were sitting in the second row.
Christian turned around to glance at the door.
He lifted up his left hand to let us know
our places in their row.
I was happy to see all of them after fifty years
of absence.

lo destroza para
privarme de sus palabras
de sus sintaxis de contradicciones

Twenty-three: Hyperemesis

There was never a graveyard for them.
They are all dead.
They never had a funeral.

The truth is we did what we could.

The cry of voices I still hear clearly
wakes me at night.
During daylight I imagine
his silhouette runs around the house,
romps with his sisters, his voice
calls for help.

The doctor was cold as the ice in my whiskey now.

The snow covered red scars and spring came
with budding trees and sunny days.

We cried for them on our own side of the bed.

de su estilística soberana
vestida de ropas coloniales
salidas de cambios violentos

Twenty-four: Balance

As a child, I thought of the world
as kind, beautiful.
I grew up naïve, protected from my own people,
the country's fears, life was fair and full of promises.
God was around.

To believe supreme forces keep equilibrium.
A war against myself.

de inquisiciones de alma,
no sólo de ideas viene esta lengua arropada
sino también de olores y caricias embrionarias

Twenty-five: For R.G.

A sharp tongue protects you from us.
You still walk with friends' knives
sticking from your back,
hands, forehead and toes.
A sound of a beast there,
the immensity of the forest extinguished,

leaving only iron walls that surround bodies,
protecting butterfly souls.

viene esta lengua majestuosa
y me convierte en una araña
que se cae de su tela

Twenty-six: Pure Math

I see you in your green Marlboro sweater
I bought in Stockholm last winter.
The last visit to a cold city.
Algorithms behind you on the blackboard.
Empty chairs in the classroom
once were full of youngsters
looking for themselves in numbers.

The effort at the corner of your lips smiling at me,
the trembling paper between your fingers. I see it all.
If I could stop time
I would do it, the awareness of a reality
you don't need.

My curiosity put you here.
I give you my heart without the black ribbons
that make me shrink.
I give you my worst, what I have left.

Don't be afraid,
find your solution, a tender word for me.
Look inside unknown numbers to find us.

me convierte en una hormiga sin monte
nn un copihue sin Sur
en una sequia sin agua

Twenty-Seven: Memories

Do you go away murmuring about sadness?
Don't go away with your silence and your Sunday laziness,
lift up your eyes and hammer them into my brain
so I can keep forever those eyes of yours.

Don't leave me without the road dust that your feet leave
because the image of those slow steps reminds me
I am not alone shedding tears like drawings in the sand.

The cold night comes, your timid silhouette
touches my senses in the cove of a forgotten port.
Your white fingers touch my shores,
the night wind stirs the trees crowded with owls
who lament your comings and goings.

Born in a port city, your life is full of
goodbyes and departures,
the uncontrollable time of
kisses and caresses flood the meeting
in the high tide of life.

Fever in distant bodies
like stones recuperating,
joy hidden as living sap.
Everything burns for a second,
water, sky. Men who were alone find at last
their common place on the earth.

Man who is desired and never forgotten,
who resists a prayer to forget,
leave your baggage and hat in this eternal waiting
of my injured door.

Take my hands and sense,
as in the long wait of these diffuse years,
your face illuminated and intact
spared from amnesia.

Recover lost time between countries
without names, tongues
without sounds, pain incarnated,
houses with naked walls, cold hands
from graves, dry kisses and bitter mouths.

Come and feel how after this long silence
my heart seeks to tell you that I am only yours.

y trepo los peldanos
del recuerdo
y de nuevo las palabras cargadas de sentido

Twenty-Eight: Details

I forgot
telephone numbers,
streets, names of trees,
even the names of the toys
I once played with.

I don't know how or when
feelings of anger, sadness, frustration cooled.
They were continually building up in the body.
– Fortunately the body doesn't keep useless things for long. –

By the grace of magic, feelings remain
of soft nostalgia, love, and passion.
I wasn't capable of getting over
all the evil and I
forgot it to survive the exile.

I wasn't capable of forgetting
the good, of erasing from my mind
images of the Chilean South.
People and places that I love.

Sometimes I think the best
that can happen to a refugee
is to remember only the
good:

to wear like a tiny brooch on the chest
all the good that Chile is as a nation.

me devuelven
la vida misma
atazcada en sonidos extranjeros

Twenty-Nine: Yellow Ribbons

I didn't like the literary staging
glorifying the young soldier,
I didn't like the mortars,
nor dying with my boots on.
I didn't like asking permission
of the shadows of the past and
the shadows of the future,
the present pouring out in songs
through the windows,
falling down in pieces from the lips,
everything on the verge of being born
in a tumult of new poetry.

What is still worth something
we carry within,
encrusted in the spider web of the dream.
The play of voices
of the conscience sings to us.
But how can we sing without voices?
How can we sing with a
knot in our throats?

It is not enough to say Yes! Now it's time!
It lacks the strength of
everyone together.
I don't like the sensation of fear,
to lose everything that was mine, everything
that was gained with sacrifice and toil.

Everyone tells me the road is long and cold,
and I shiver to see what was simple and pure
run away like water in a chain of mountains.

My skin is curdled with hope,
thinking that we got far and we learned
from the most unexpected lesson:
I still have the glare of the sun in the morning.

*el lenguaje casi muerto
me revive y me envuelve
en su manto de sol y sombra
de agua y hielo y así*

Thirty: Just in Time

For José Miguel Cruz

The night before your call, I dreamt of the ocean:
Cold, dangerous, deep, dark, blue at dusk and dawn.

Taking a big breath, I left my body in this building
in the North for the Southern Hemisphere.

I fell into the arms of aunts and sisters
preparing a Sunday table, bountiful with
corn pie, tomato salad, green beans
and onions with cilantro,
thousand-layer cake and port from the Santa Rita vineyard.

I saw my nieces and nephews
laughing with pleasure that lasted centuries.

The sweet, bitter, sandy taste of an oyster with lemon
reminded me of a place I was willing to die for.

I felt as if I didn't have a destiny,
I thought effort was not enough,
as if their lives were in vain.

It is clear to me, fights like this
are all won long before they are fought.
Where exactly?

At a Sunday table?
On a dark empty road that hides subversion?
In the kindness we summon, stirring the lawlessness within ourselves?

Thanks for your call.

me convierte en ese Yo de siempre
y me subyugo como esclava
bajo su dominio
enamorada
per secula seculorum.

Conclusion

Life begins when we replace
what is dead.
A simple regeneration of the cells.

GUESTHOUSE

Hair of Sand

Out of the lost memories
she is getting closer
little by little
half awake
and full of dust
comes
my mother tongue
to bring me
pleasant memories
violent smells
timid words
whispers of a man
in my ears
bells in an open sea
winds from the south and white lilies
comes my mother tongue
charged with nostalgia
as always
to leave me
a package of rainy days
warm bodies
in front of a fireplace
she comes calmed with her hair of sand
with her mouth of ocean
with her caresses in the darkness
she comes and sings me her verses
to calm my sadness
she comes sweet and strong
with syllables I recognize
with delicious sounds
with voices like a stream
she comes and I bow in homage
as to a queen in her palace
I give her my most
precious treasures
phrases of lament
fresh laughter
a bouquet of violets bought in Huérfanos
the air of the Ocean

the black sand of San Pedro
the robust whistle of the wind
the dark red of
the dusk in Santiago
words of love whispered
and again the sound of the Ocean
on Quiriquina Island
the rumble of a sea shell
before the arrival of the soldiers
the sound of an island
without torture chambers and the handsome
young Captain approaching my cousin
the first kiss in the high school
on the bank of the Mapocho River
across the Forestal Park
this giant tongue comes
and sweeps away my body
she submerges me in the sounds
of human catastrophies
she sweeps away my heart
with a bloody knife
she destroys to deny me
her words
her syntax of contradictions
her sovereign stylistics
of colonial clothes
and violent changes
inquisitions of the soul
this tongue comes not only dressed with ideas
but with scent and embryonic caresses
this majestic tongue
converts me into a spider
that falls from her web
she converts me into
an ant without a hill
into a Chilean bellflower without the "South"
into a well without water
and I climb up the steps
of reminiscence and again
the words charged with meaning
return me to life itself

trapped in foreign sounds
the language almost dead
revives me and wraps me
in her cape of sun and shadows
of water and ice and so
I become myself
and I subjugate myself as a slave
in love
under her dominion
for ever and ever.

Notes:

This poetry collection, *HOUSE*, is dedicated entirely to my grandfather Primitivo Vera Coloma.

"Poem Without a Number: House" is dedicated to Julio Santibañez.

"Poem Nine: On a Quiet Summer's Night" is dedicated to my grandmother Elena Astorga Saravia.

Quiriquina, Tejas Verdes, República, Villa Grimaldi, The Parral House were torture chambers built by the Chilean Secret Police during the Augusto Pinochet regime.

"Two: Poems That Contradict Each Other" is based on the movie *Nacht und Nebel,* shown in the U.S. under the title *Night and Fog.* This 1955 documentary film about political prisoners during World War II was shot covertly by French film-maker Alain Resnais, who was able to obtain some of the most disturbing footage ever shown of prisoners and victims in the camps in World War II. The film focuses primarily on questions of hate and human responsibility. The title *Nacht und Nebel* was based on the title Jean Cayrol, an escapee from Mauthausen, used in his memoir, *Poèmes de la nuit et brouillard* (1946).

The Spanish stanzas that run at the bottom of each page become an English voice in *Guesthouse*, the second part of the book.

About the Author

Mariela Griffor is the author of *Exiliana* (Luna Publications) and *House* (Mayapple Press). She was born in the city of Concepción in southern Chile. She attended the University of Santiago and the Catholic University of Rio de Janeiro. She left Chile for an involuntary exile in Sweden in 1985. She lives in Grosse Pointe Park, Michigan. She is founder of the Institute for Creative Writers at Wayne State University and Publisher of Marick Press. Her work has appeared in periodicals across Latin America and the United States. Mariela holds a B.A in Journalism and a M.A. in Media Studies from Wayne State University. She is Honorary Consul of Chile in Michigan.

Other recent titles from Mayapple Press:

John Repp, *Fever*, 2007
        Paper, 36 pp, $11.95 plus s&h
        ISBN 978-0932412-522

Kathryn Kirkpatrick, *Out of the Garden*, 2007
        Paper, 80 pp, $14.95 plus s&h
        ISBN 978-0932412-515

Gerry LaFemina, *The Book of Clown Baby/Figures from the Big Time Circus Book*, 2007
        Paper, 60 pp, $14.95 plus s&h
        ISBN 978-0932412-508

Nancy Botkin, *Parts That Were Once Whole*, 2007
        Paper, 72 pp, $14.95 plus s&h
        ISBN 978-0932412-492

David Lunde, *Instead*, 2007
        Paper, 72 pp, $14.95 plus s&h
        ISBN 978-0932412-485

Zilka Joseph, *Lands I Live In*, 2007
        Paper, 42 pp, $12.95 plus s&h
        ISBN 978-0932412-478

Johanny Vásquez Paz, *Poemas Callejeros/Streetwise Poems*, 2007
        Paper, 74 pp, $14.95 plus s&h
        ISBN 978-0932412-461

Larry Levy, *I Would Stay Forever If I Could and New Poems*, 2007
        Paper, 60 pp, $12.95 plus s&h
        ISBN 0-932412-45-9

Christine Hamm, *The Transparent Dinner*, 2006
        Paper, 90 pp, $15.95 plus s&h
        ISBN 0-932412-44-0

Kathleen Tyler, *The Secret Box*, 2006
        Paper, 74 pp, $14.95 plus s&h
        ISBN 0-932412-43-2

Rachel Eshed, *Little Promises*, 2006 (bilingual Hebrew/English)
        Paper, 104 pp, $16 plus s&h
        ISBN 0-932412-42-4

For a complete catalog of Mayapple Press publications, please visit our website at *www.mayapplepress.com*. Books can be ordered direct from our website with secure on-line payment using PayPal, or by mail (check or money order). Or order through your local bookseller.